SPORTS PARABLES

COACHING
KINGDOM PRINCIPLES
THROUGH SPORTS

RON BROWN

WITH CHAD BONHAM
FOREWORD BY GORDON THIESSEN

Sports Parables

Ron Brown with Chad Bonham

ISBN 978-1-938254-75-8

Cross Training Publishing

15418 Weir Street #177

Omaha, NE 68137

(308) 293-3891

www.crosstrainingpublishing.com

www.kingdomsports.online

FOREWORD BY GORDON THIESSEN

I met Ron Brown 32 years ago at a coaches clinic in Lincoln, NE. I was serving as the area representative in Central and Western Nebraska for the Fellowship of Christian Athletes. We were the same age and had both played college football. We also shared the same passion for reaching the state of Nebraska with the gospel, using the platform of sports. I always felt privileged to introduce him each spring to Husker fans around the state as we traveled to his speaking engagements.

He especially loved driving through the sandhills and listening to fans talk about everything from milking cows to castrating bulls. On one day, I scheduled him to speak at six different places and nearly killed him! He still gives me a hard time about that. His boldness to share the gospel throughout the state has never wavered for a single moment.

He understood the opportunity God had given him to use his platform as a Husker football coach in a football-crazed state to tell people about Jesus.

After nearly 30 years of serving with the FCA in Nebraska, it was my privilege to co-found Kingdom Sports with Ron Brown. Things we taught together during those years we have now put into books, radio shows, podcasts, and videos at www.kingdomsports.online.

This book is an accumulation of 32 years of reading the Bible and coaching young men each week on the gridiron for Coach Brown. You will find these parables and lessons to be life changing. They're not just for coaches, athletes or sports fans; anyone who reads this book will be more excited about reading God's Word and serving King Jesus.

TABLE OF CONTENTS

INTRODUCTION BY RON BROWN

Our world is filled with stories. Whether we're telling one, reading one, hearing one or watching one, there's something mysteriously irresistible about a great story. Our lives, in fact, are one big story that is unfolding before our very eyes.

Maybe that's why Jesus used so many stories in His teachings. Sometimes He used them as a tool to explain the gospel to the unbeliever who didn't understand. He also used parables to convict hardened hearts like those of the Pharisees and Scribes who did not want to hear the truth. (Matthew 13:11-15) Other times, He used them to clarify and bring depth and color to the believer who did understand.

Jesus' stories were called parables. If you break down that word you'll see the Greek prefix "para," which means to come alongside something and magnify truth. That's what made them so powerful. That's why they were also used often throughout the teachings from the early church.

The apostle Paul, for instance, talks about common people in society like farmers and soldiers to convey uncommon principles. He even invoked athletic imagery to make deep spiritual truths.

Do you not know that in a race all the runners run, but only one gets the prize? Run in such a way as to get the prize. Everyone who competes in the games goes into strict training. They do it to get a crown that will not last, but we do it to get a crown that will last forever. Therefore I do not run like someone running aimlessly; I do not fight like a boxer beating the air. (1 Corinthians 9:24-26)

Parables and analogies are still used today. Educators and communicators understand how they help people learn and retain information. You see them used in textbooks and on standardized tests like the ACT and the SAT.

In nearly 40 years as a coach I've observed this truth in action, and that's why I use stories and analogies on a regular basis when speaking to athletes, coaches and parents. I call them **Sports Parables**.

With this book, our goal is to use these parables to differentiate between the Kingdom of God and the Kingdom of man. We want to give believers learnable ways to digest that truth, which is using the world you live in to help define that truth. We also want to help coaches introduce the gospel to their athletes.

The concepts found in **Sports Parables** use relevant terminology and things commonly taught in practice and throughout the course of competition to bring greater knowledge, wisdom and understanding regarding spiritual things.

Use the parables in your teaching. Use them in your coaching. Use them in your discipleship and mentoring. Use them in your personal Bible studies or in a Bible study group.

You can also go to our website, **kingdomsports.online**, and watch our videos that show these parables in action. Some of the highlighted drills have been replicated at middle schools, high schools, and college campuses across the country.

Many of these parables are related to my field of expertise, football. Some are related to general sports concepts such as training or team building. If they don't transfer directly to your sport, I encourage you to get creative and find ways to translate the concepts to your athletes. I also hope you will be inspired to come up with sports parables of your own if you aren't already doing so.

Thank you for taking the time to read **Sports Parables**. We're excited you've decided to join us on this journey as we work together to share the gospel and make disciples as we fulfill our call to build the Kingdom of God!

1

~~~~~~

CHAPTER ONE

FIRST STEP

A Parable About New Beginnings

> **"Therefore, if anyone is in Christ, the new creation has come: The old has gone, the new is here!" – Apostle Paul**

In sports and in life, we hear a lot about finishing strong. Yes, finishing strong is something we should all strive to do in competition and in our personal affairs. It's the first steps taken, however, they are vitally important and will set the tone for what follows.

This is true if we're talking about friendship, marriage, parenting, business, education, health, or any other venture imaginable. Success and failure are often determined from the very beginning.

FIRST STEP

There's no question that a strong first step is important across many athletic disciplines.

Baseball and softball players want to take a strong, quick first step out of the batter's box after making contact with the ball.

Basketball players handling the ball need to take a strong first step when making an offensive move toward the basket.

Tennis players must engage a decisive first step when returning serves or charging to make a play at the net.

Soccer, lacrosse, hockey, volleyball and track athletes also require a solid first step in order to be successful in competition. It's a vital component of so many different sports.

Of course, this is also true in football. We always taught our players the importance of their first step on any assignment. We worked diligently on this concept with a variety of position players including running backs, blocking backs, quarterbacks and defensive backs.

While working with receivers, I constantly preached about the importance of taking a hard but quick first step as they either began their routes or exploded from the line of scrimmage to block a defender. That first step inevitably would be the difference between getting a jump on the cornerback or getting clogged up in his route.

Finishing strong is the goal, but it's hard to do that if you don't start with a strong first step.

NAME CHANGER

In the months following the ascension of Christ, the early Church quickly grew in number and spread across the region like wildfire. Not everyone was excited about this development.

One of the dissenters was a powerful Jewish leader named Saul of Tarsus. He was violently against the conversion of Jews to the Christian faith, so much so that he was rounding up new believers and imprisoning them. Saul even watched in approval as a young convert and aspiring apostle named Stephen was stoned to death for blasphemy.

Saul believed he was doing God's work. He had authority, influence and momentum. That all changed as he neared the city of Damascus where he planned to continue his efforts to persecute the Christians.

As he neared Damascus on his journey, suddenly a light from heaven flashed around him. He fell to the ground and heard a voice say to him, "Saul, Saul, why do you persecute me?"

"Who are you, Lord?" Saul asked.

"I am Jesus, whom you are persecuting," he replied. "Now get up and go into the city, and you will be told what you must do."

The men traveling with Saul stood there speechless; they heard the sound but did not see anyone. Saul got up from the ground, but when he opened his eyes he could see nothing. So they led him by the hand into Damascus. (Acts 9:3-8)

Saul remained blind for the next three days. He also refused to eat or drink. That's when the Lord told a believer named Ananias to heal Saul of his blindness and proclaim the gospel of Christ. On that day, this man who once persecuted Christians was filled with the Holy Spirit, baptized in water and set forth down a new path. It was a strong first step in a new direction that would change the world forever.

As time passed, Saul became known as Paul. Some theologians believe this name was used to help him be more relatable to the non-Jewish people he was evangelizing. Others believe the name was meant to indicate a fresh start, a departure from his ugly past.

No matter the reason, Paul ascended as one of the early Church's greatest apostles. He even wrote nearly one-third of the New Testament in the form of letters to believers in cities such as Rome, Galatia, Colossae, Thessalonica and Ephesus.

Paul never would have become a transformative figure in our history, however, had he not been brought to his knees and forced to make a life-altering decision. New beginnings aren't always easy, but the results can be incredibly impactful and rewarding.

NEW BEGINNINGS

There's an expiration date attached to an athlete's pursuits for competitive excellence. At some point, the games will end. And while taking a strong first step might be temporarily beneficial to an athlete, a strong first step in the spiritual realm will change a person's eternal future.

You will make many decisions throughout your life. You'll decide where to go to school, who to marry, when to start a family, when to start or change a career and how to prepare for retirement. There are lots of ways to start strong, whether though education, counseling, planning or saving.

The alternative is doing it on your own and risking the likelihood of a shaky, slow, tentative or downright bad start. A bad start will slow you down. A bad start will take you off course. A bad start will lead you toward destruction and possibly the end of whatever you are pursuing.

That doesn't mean you can't get back on track or finally get to your destination, but a bad start can make it more difficult and create unnecessary challenges and obstacles that ultimately keep you from getting there on time.

There is no stronger first step you can take, however, than to fall on your knees and ask the Holy Spirit for guidance in every decision to make. You should never start a new venture without Christ. He is the ultimate source of new beginnings.

"I am the Alpha and the Omega," says the Lord God, "who is, and who was, and who is to come, the Almighty." (Revelation 1:8)

It doesn't end there. What if you've had a tough day? Let's say things didn't go right. You can always go back to the beginning of that day or back to when you first trusted in Christ. He will refresh you again if you keep going back to Him. Every morning, you get a chance to wake up and take in the breath God has given you.

Because of the LORD's great love we are not consumed,for his compassions never fail. They are new every morning; great is your faithfulness. (Lamentations 3:22-23)

There are three things we can do to take that fresh step every day.

1) Walk with Him. Daily conversations with Jesus through the vehicle of prayer are life giving. We gain strength for the journey and wisdom for the day when we spend quality time talking to and listening to the Lord. We draw closer to Him, and He purifies our hearts.

Let us draw near to God with a sincere heart and with the full assurance that faith brings, having our hearts sprinkled to cleanse us from a guilty conscience and having our bodies washed with pure water. (Hebrews 10:22)

2) Study His Word. Don't just read the Bible. Study it. Break it down. Ask wise Christians to help you understand its never changing principles.

Do your best to present yourself to God as one approved, a worker who does not need to be ashamed and who correctly handles the word of truth. (2 Timothy 2;15)

3) Worship Him. There is so much power in telling the Lord how much you love and adore Him. If you start your day with praise in your heart and on your lips and worship him even while you compete, you'll be amazed at how much differently you view the cares of life.

Sing to the LORD a new song; sing to the LORD, all the earth. Sing to the LORD, praise his name; proclaim his salvation day after day Declare his glory among the nations, his marvelous deeds among all peoples. (Psalm 96:1-3)

None of this is possible, however, if you don't take the ultimate first step and give your heart to Christ. You must fully surrender to Him and submit to Him as Lord of your life. The apostle Paul understood this because he experienced it in a powerful way.

Therefore, if anyone is in Christ, the new creation has come: The old has gone, the new is here! (2 Corinthians 5:17)

Christ gave us a brand new beginning. We are born again through the spirit of God. When we give our lives to Christ and repent of our sins and trust in Him as our Savior and Lord, He starts a brand new life in us. He promises us access to His mercy and His grace. There is no stronger first step than to daily commit to living our lives for Jesus.

STUDY QUESTIONS

1. Give an example of what a strong first step looks like in your sport. Why is it so important you succeed? What happens if you take a bad or weak first step?

2. Describe a time when you had a new beginning in your life. Do you feel like you got off to a strong start or a weak start? How did that first step impact you later on?

3. What is your initial takeaway from Saul's story? How do you think his first steps after his encounter with Jesus set the tone for the rest of his life?

4. Where are you currently in your relationship with God? Are you running strong, needing to go back to the starting line, or not running at all?

5. Looking back at the three ways you can get a strong start with Jesus every day, which ones are you doing well and with which ones are you struggling? How do you think improving in those areas might strengthen your daily Christian walk?

Have you believed in Jesus, repented of your sins and asked Him to become Lord of Your life? If so, praise God! You are already experiencing new life in Him! If not, please consider making that commitment so you can experience fullness of life and receive the promise of eternity in Heaven. Visit www.gty.org and listen to the sermon series "What Must I Do To Be Saved" for additional teaching.

2

~~~~~~

LOCK THE ROCK

A Parable About Securing The Gospel

> **"Gentlemen, it is better to die a small boy than to fumble this football."**
> **– John Heisman**

Most people don't know much about John Heisman, but football fans are very familiar with his last name, which graces college football's most coveted individual award—the Heisman Trophy.

Ironically, Heisman didn't gain notoriety because of his athletic ability but rather his exploits as an innovative coach at places like Auburn, Clemson, Penn, Rice, and most famously, Georgia Tech, where he won the 1917 National Championship. Equally known for his fiercely competitive nature, Heisman had a strong dislike for those moments when his players made costly mistakes like fumbling the football.

As coaches, it drives us crazy when a turnover costs us an opportunity to put points on the scoreboard and gives the opponent the ball. That's why we constantly preach the concept of ball security to our players. Simply put, you can't score if you drop the ball.

Take this scenario as an example. The ball is placed on the two-yard line. The running back takes the handoff from quarterback, jumps over the line of scrimmage, and falls into the end zone. There's just one problem. A defensive lineman applied just the right amount of pressure at just the right point of contact and forced the ball out of the running back's arms. The running back landed in the end zone, but the ball was back at the one-yard line. No ball. No touchdown.

LOCK THE ROCK

Coaches have a variety of ways to teach ball security, but they often revolve around the five points of contact: the lower bicep, the forearm, the palm, the fingers, and the chest. If the player has taken care of those points of contact, it should look like they are "pledging allegiance" to the ball.

Some coaches have even attempted to teach this concept away from the field. One common technique is to have players carry the football everywhere they go, telling them they are not allowed to put it down at any time: not in the classroom, not at the lunch table, and not even while taking a nap. This helps them understand just how vital ball security is to the team's success.

And there's more to it than just teaching a player how to protect the ball or "lock the rock," as I like to say. It's also about helping them realize there's a defensive player on the other side who wants to tear that ball away and steal the victory.

Ball security only happens when the player understands his responsibility, recognizes his enemy and commits himself to protecting that ball with everything he's got.

THE GREAT COMMISSION

After Jesus died on the cross and was resurrected from the grave, He spent 40 days teaching and fellowshipping with His followers. Just before He ascended back into Heaven, Jesus gave His team some last minute instructions:

"I have been given all authority in heaven and on earth. Therefore, go and make disciples of all the nations, baptizing them in the name of the Father and the Son and the Holy Spirit. Teach these new disciples to obey all the commands I have given you. And be sure of this: I am with you always, even to the end of the age." (Matthew 28:18-20/NLT)

Originally known as Jesus' disciples, these 11 men and a few others were given a huge responsibility. It later became known as "The

Great Commission." In that moment, Jesus was acting as the quarterback who had essentially handed his players the ball – the gospel message. They became known as the apostles, and the goal line was literally the entire world.

Just like a running back leaping into the end zone, they held tightly to the gospel. They locked the rock and took it everywhere they went. How could they fulfill Jesus' command otherwise?

The apostles also had to beware of the enemy. Satan desperately wanted to snuff out the Good News from being spread. He wanted to deny God the victory. Satan fostered great opposition that came from religious leaders, political figures, and even the king and his representatives. He used them all to try to rip the ball from the apostles' hands and end the game for good.

Satan eventually took extreme measures. He ratcheted up anger against the apostles. This led to persecution in the form of imprisonment, torture, and ultimately, death.

Can you imagine where our world would be if those men and women of God had dropped the ball? What if they had given up? What if they had decided it was too hard and left the gospel at the doorsteps of their neighbors' homes or at the entryway of the palaces and the prisons?

Thankfully they didn't drop the ball. They exercised what we might refer to as "spiritual ball security." They endured immense suffering in the process so we could have hope and an eternal future.

SECURING THE GOSPEL

When you look at a football, it's interesting to notice that the stitches run both vertically and horizontally. The visual image is amazingly similar to the shape of a cross. That's an incredible reminder as a coach or as an athlete of what it means to carry the ball—the gospel of Jesus Christ—securely and consistently everywhere you go.

What good is a Christian who has been entrusted with the gospel at a school or in a place of business if he or she has left the gospel at the doorstep? What good is a Christian who is ashamed to bring the truth of the gospel into every aspect of his or her life?

We need to remind ourselves that we can't be an effective witness for Christ if we leave the ball at the doorstep of our offices, at our churches, at our homes, or at our huddle groups. We need to share that message with our players as well. The ball is representative of the gospel. We can never let it out of our sight or set it down. We must lock the rock and take it everywhere we go.

Otherwise, it's like leaping into the end zone but leaving the ball at the one-yard line. It doesn't really count.

STUDY QUESTIONS

1. What are some techniques and concepts you use to teach your athletes about ball security?

2. Is spiritual ball security (taking the gospel everywhere you go) something you find difficult? Explain.

3. What are some ways you can demonstrate this concept to your players through your example, your actions, your testimony, etc.?

4. Go back and read Matthew 28:18-20. What personal application can you make from this passage?

5. How do you hope the concept of spiritual ball security might impact your players and help them become more effective witnesses for Christ?

3

~~~~~

CHEESE IN A MOUSETRAP

A Parable About Deception

> # "The essence of football was blocking, tackling, and execution based on timing, rhythm and deception." – Knute Rockne

In 1918, an already popular football player turned coach took the reins at the University of Notre Dame. Knute Rockne led the program for 13 dominant seasons that resulted in 105 wins and three national championships.

Even though football was still a relatively young sport, Rockne understood success required misdirection, disguised schemes, and the element of surprise—or as he plainly stated "timing, rhythm and deception."

Ironically, many of his popular concepts (such as the famous Notre Dame Box) originated from the innovative mind of Amos Alonzo Stagg, who happened to be one of America's first prominent Christian coaches. Stagg began coaching in 1890 and was famous for inventing sneaky plays such as the end-around, the line shift, the man in motion, and the quick kick. Deception has increasingly become more prominent in football ever since.

I played safety during my college career at Brown University and remember constantly being on the lookout for offenses using disguised protections. For instance, when I would see uncovered linemen and tight ends positioned to block, that meant I needed to switch from a pass defender to a run responsibility guy.

There were times, however, when those linemen and tight ends kept low pads to make it look like it was going to be a run play when it was really going to be a play action pass. At that point, I had to be aware that the wide receivers and tight ends might be going out for a pass.

The play looked like a run. It smelled like a run. It even acted like a run. But it wasn't really a run. It was a pass. And if I didn't sniff it out or if I took the bait, the quarterback was going to throw over the top of me for a touchdown.

CHEESE IN A MOUSETRAP

Disguised protections are a lot like cheese in a mousetrap. Just like the mouse is easily tempted to go after that delicious, aromatic morsel, a defensive back can easily be tempted to blitz the line in the hopes of dropping the running back for a loss.

The mouse has to recognize that the cheese might taste good for a moment, but it's probably going to cost him his life. The defensive back might occasionally guess correctly, but you can guarantee he'll be having a long conversation with his coach on the sideline when he guesses wrong.

If temptation is one of deception's biggest lures, then knowledge and wisdom are two of deception's biggest cures. Take for instance the Royal Canadian Mounted Police and their vigilance against counterfeit currency. When they inspect money coming through the border they're often easily able to spot the fake bills, not because they've studied the counterfeits but rather because they've intently studied the accurate currency. They know it so well that when something is just a little bit off, they can spot it.

There are too many counterfeits to study them all, but there's one accurate currency. That's what they study. That's how they know the difference.

That same mentality separates the great defensive back from the good defensive back. The great defensive back studies hours of film and watches for the little things in the opposing team's offensive schemes. That's how he can recognize when a pass play is disguised as a run play. He's watched the film. He's trained for that moment. His dedication has allowed him to perform his function with authority.

GOOD TO THE EYE

One of the most tragic Bible stories takes place very early in human history. Found in Genesis 3, we read the account of Adam and Eve, earth's first man and woman, and how they fell prey to one of the great deceptions ever.

It all happened in a moment when Adam and Eve were alone in the Garden of Eden—a perfect habitat God had created for them. God had given Adam and Eve permission to eat fruit from any tree except the one in the middle. Satan also occupied the garden. He knew about God's rule and took up the form of a snake in order to trick them into disobeying the Creator.

"You will not certainly die," the serpent said to the woman. "For God knows that when you eat from it your eyes will be opened, and you will be like God, knowing good and evil." When the woman saw that the fruit of the tree was good for food and pleasing to the eye, and also desirable for gaining wisdom, she took some and ate it. She also gave some to her husband, who was with her, and he ate it. (vv. 4-6)

Instantly, their eyes were opened to the reality of good and evil. And instantly Adam and Eve realized their guilt. They were tempted to eat the fruit because it looked good to the eye. They were tempted by the lure of being like God. It was all too easy.

Adam and Eve were also tempted because they listened to Satan's counterfeit message. Even though they had walked with God, they were not able to discern the difference between truth and lies. Their sin caused them to be separated from God and removed from the garden. That separation from God would last for thousands of years until the arrival of Jesus Christ, who would sacrifice His life to pay for our sins.

Death and destruction entered into this world because two people gave in to the deception of lust and pride. Today, we continue to fight against that deception as the enemy attempts to separate us from God and pull us away from the God-given purpose and plan for our lives.

AVOIDING DECEPTION

As believers, we have the daily choice to accept the truth and live by that truth, or we can listen to the enemy and give in to his lies. Unfortunately, we've seen the vast majority of mankind doing the latter since the beginning of time. Jesus even tells us there will be mass deception as we approach the end of the age (Matthew 24:24). There will be false prophets. There will be teachings that sound good to the ears but have nothing to do with sound biblical principles.

How does the believer overcome this? How do we protect ourselves from deception?

1. Study His Word. You have to be willing to study the scriptures so well that you can spot a counterfeit gospel. We also get wisdom, reproof and correction from the Word of God.

"But as for you, continue in what you have learned and have become convinced of, because you know those from whom you learned it, and how from infancy you have known the Holy Scriptures, which are able to make you wise for salvation through faith in Christ Jesus." *(2 Timothy 3:14-15)*

2. Know His Voice. As we get deeper in God's Word, we'll be better able to hear and discern His voice, which comes through the scriptures and through the Holy Spirit working in our lives.

"My sheep listen to my voice; I know them, and they follow me. I give them eternal life, and they shall never perish; no one will snatch them out of my hand." (John 10:27-28)

3. Root Out Pride. As athletes and coaches, it's far too easy to give in to the temptation to get the glory after making the big play or winning the big game. That's all a product of pride, which is the most destructive force in human history. Instead, we should focus on giving our best and doing everything in excellence with the purpose of giving God the glory.

"For all those who exalt themselves will be humbled, and those who humble themselves will be exalted." (Luke 14:11)

STUDY QUESTIONS

1. Can you give an example of a time when you were tricked into making a mistake during competition? What were the consequences of your mistake?

2. What are some other ways an athletic opponent might try to deceive you into giving them a competitive advantage?

3. In what circumstances do you typically find yourself susceptible to spiritual deception?

4. Which do you find most difficult: knowing God's Word, knowing God's voice, or rooting out pride in your life? Explain.

5. What are some things you can begin doing today that will help you fight against the enemy's attempts to deceive you and draw you away from God's plan for your life?

4

~~~~~~

CHAPTER FOUR

COMING BACK TO THE BALL

A Parable About Discipleship

"Nobody who ever gave his best regretted it." – George Halas

George Halas is known as one of the NFL's hardest nosed coaches. His consistent demand for excellence produced some of the game's toughest players and teams. Over a 40-year span, Halas led the Chicago Bears to eight NFL championships. Many of his players are still considered among the franchise's elite including Dick Butkus: Mike Ditka, Paddy Driscoll, Red Grange, Sid Luckman, Bronco Nagurski, Gayle Sayers, George Trafton and Bulldog Turner.

I can imagine it drove Halas crazy when any of his players lacked aggressiveness and drive. Most coaches still share that frustration, myself included. There's not much worse than watching athletes who play tentatively or give less than 100 percent effort.

We see this in every sport. Baseball and softball players might lackadaisically let a grounder come to them instead of charging the ball. Basketball players might stand in the corner waiting for the pass instead of setting a pick or making a strong move to get open. Volleyball players might decide to let a ball float out of reach instead of making a diving play. Tennis players might sit back on the baseline waiting for the opponent to make a mistake instead of going for a winner.

How an athlete handles everything from the routine to the spectacular says a lot of his mindset. Do they have a sense of urgency or are they hum ho in their approach? Ultimately it's about excellence, and you can't be excellent if you're not giving your best effort. Taking it back a step, you can't give your best effort if you haven't properly trained for those moments.

Like Halas once conveyed, there's no regret when you give your best.

There's no downside to becoming the best athlete you can be. It's up to the athlete to make that decision and work hard daily to achieve that end.

COMING BACK TO THE BALL

As a football coach, one of my biggest pet peeves was when receivers didn't come back to the ball. In those moments, it revealed some shortcomings my players needed to work through. Either they were unsure of the route and didn't know where to expect the ball or they simply didn't care enough to fight for it.

When a pass is thrown, the receiver has to be thinking, "That's my ball!" You can be assured the coach has been preaching to them all week during practice not to wait on the ball.

Geometry and physics tell you that while you're motionless, someone else is in motion and is going to arrive at an angle where they might be able to intercept or deflect the ball before you get there. That's why the receiver has to shorten the distance between himself and the ball, and many times that means shaving the angle and coming back to make the catch.

On any given play, the hungrier guy is going to get the job done. The lax receiver isn't fighting to get open. The unmotivated receiver isn't shortening the distance of the passing lane.

Focus is also important. The distracted receiver isn't looking for the ball. He's distracted by looking at the cheerleaders or fans in the stands.

It all starts, however, with training and practice. That's where a motivated receiver listens to his coach and follows his instructions while the entitled receiver assumes he is talented enough to go through the motions and then somehow magically be ready to perform on game day.

SPIRITUAL HUNGER

After Jesus rose from the dead, He spent 40 days teaching and encouraging His disciples before ascending into heaven. The leadership amongst the group, now referred to as apostles, assembled in Jerusalem to await the arrival of the Holy Spirit, which Jesus had promised would come and serve as their comforter, their strength and their guide.

In Acts 2, there's an amazing scene that takes place. First of all, the Holy Spirit comes in a powerful and unusual way that empowers the apostles to share the gospel with the thousands of Jewish people who were in Jerusalem celebrating Shauvot or the "Feast of Weeks."

The apostles had gathered in an upper room when the Holy Spirit made a supernatural entrance. The sound of a violent wind came through the house and "tongues of fire" rested on each of them. The Holy Spirit gave them the ability to speak in other languages and they went out into the city to use this incredible ability to share the gospel with people from many nations.

This eventful scene is now referred to as the Day of Pentecost and marks the birth of the Church, as about 3,000 people repented of their sins and believed in Christ.

That was just the beginning. The apostles and new believers didn't stop there. They weren't satisfied with just being on the team. It was time to go deeper. It was time to grow. It was time to spread the gospel even further and to more people. Their next actions are often referred to as "The Fellowship of the Believers."

They devoted themselves to the apostles' teaching and to fellowship, to the breaking of bread and to prayer. Everyone was filled with awe at the many wonders and signs performed by the apostles. All the believers were together and had everything in common. They sold property and possessions to give to anyone who had need. Every day they continued to meet together in the temple courts. They

*broke bread in their homes and ate together with glad and sincere
hearts, praising God and enjoying the favor of all the people. And
the Lord added to their number daily those who were being saved.
(Acts 2:42-47)*

Even though they faced great opposition and even persecution that
often led to torture and death, the early Christians committed themselves to their own spiritual growth and to the discipleship of every
new convert to the faith.

THE CALL TO DISCIPLESHIP

Just like in athletics, our Christian walk requires training, focus,
dedication and an aggressive desire to grow in our faith. That means
being intentional about coming back to the Word of God and foster-
ing an attitude of spiritual hunger. It's called discipleship, and it's a
process in which every believer is called to engage.

Discipleship starts in our private time and extends to our public ex-
pressions, but it's worth it when we see how growing closer to Jesus
can transform our lives and the lives around us.

1. Read God's Word. If you don't wake up each day with a plan to
study God's Word, you can't become a doer of the Word. Not understanding the scriptures also opens the door to the enemy who wants
to intercept the gospel and take it away from you.

*All Scripture is inspired by God and is useful to teach us what is
true and to make us realize what is wrong in our lives. It corrects us
when we are wrong and teaches us to do what is right. God uses it
to prepare and equip his people to do every good work. (2 Timothy
3:16-17)*

2. Spend time in prayer. Just like an athlete can't truly know his
coach without ever speaking to him, believers must also communicate with the One who has all the answers to our questions and all

the solutions to our problems. There is real power in talking to and listening to the Lord.

And pray in the Spirit on all occasions with all kinds of prayers and requests. With this in mind, be alert and always keep on praying for all the Lord's people. (Ephesians 6:18)

3. Fellowship with the believers. Being a part of the local church is a vital part of the discipleship process. We need to submit to pastoral authority and pay close attention as they rightly divide the Word of Truth.

And let us consider how we may spur one another on toward love and good deeds, not giving up meeting together, as some are in the habit of doing, but encouraging one another—and all the more as you see the Day approaching. (Hebrews 10:24-25)

4. Open yourself to accountability. We all need someone to keep us on track. This means being open to wise, trustworthy counsel from believers who have shown themselves to be knowledgeable in the scriptures and are willing to ask you tough questions.

Dear brothers and sisters, if another believer is overcome by some sin, you who are godly should gently and humbly help that person back onto the right path. And be careful not to fall into the same temptation yourself. (Galatians 6:1)

If you make the intentional effort to undergo the discipleship process you won't regret it, and the spiritual dividends will be much greater and far more eternally significant than anything we can work toward in this life.

STUDY QUESTIONS

1. On a scale of 1-10 (1 being very passive, 10 being very aggressive), how would you rank your playing or coaching style? What factors play into your assessment?

2. After reading about the early Church in Acts 2, what are some of its notable characteristics that stand out to you?

3. In terms of spiritual matters, what does "coming back to the ball" mean to you?

4. Look back at the four steps in the discipleship process. Which of those things are you doing well? Which of those things are you struggling to do consistently?

5. What can you start doing today that will help you be more aggressive in your desire to grow closer to the Lord?

5

~~~~~~~~

CHAPTER FIVE

THE
PERSECUTORS

A Parable About Fear

"Fatigue makes cowards of us all."
– Vince Lombardi

There's no doubt about it. Vince Lombardi is one of the greatest coaches in NFL history. It's hard to argue with success, and Lombardi's run with the Green Bay Packers was loaded with results. He won six NFL championships, the first two Super Bowls, and finished his career with a .738 winning percentage.

His famous quotes, however, are almost as legendary as his iconic achievements, and there's one in particular that has always stood out to me. "Fatigue makes cowards of us all."

There is so much truth in that six-word sentence. Not only do we become fearful when we are physically tired, but we also allow fear to creep in when we are emotionally, mentally and spiritually tired. Any one of those manifestations can be disastrous for both the athlete and the follower of Christ.

THE PERSECUTORS

As a coach, I want to identify fear in my players. I'm not exposing their fear so I can publicly embarrass them and call them cowards. I'm exposing it gently. I'm showing them how they have allowed fatigue to reveal their fear during practice and during games.

In some cases I've been able to point out these issues through game film. Most of the time, however, I prefer to do so through practice drills like one called "The Persecutors." In it, the receivers run a short route, catch a pass and then are immediately greeted by two defenders holding hand shields ready to make contact to force the receiver off his route or, better yet, force him to cough up the ball.

As the defenders get more aggressive, it's amazing to see how quickly the receivers lose focus and start thinking about the hit instead of first catching the ball and then fighting for extra yards. Sometimes they won't even catch the ball. The thought of resistance can cause the receivers to come across the field with alligator arms, which is a half-hearted effort to not fully extend their arms. Balls are dropped all over the place.

There's another drill I've used during practice and at football camps in which the athletes run toward me at full speed from about 20 or 30 yards away. As they cut the distance between us in half, I fire a pass right at them. It's amazing to see how the kids respond. They usually slow down or flinch. The drill exposes their fear. They're either afraid of the ball hurting their hands or afraid of dropping the ball.

There are plenty of ways fear can be exposed in other sports as well. For instance, a coach might blare loud music during basketball, baseball, softball or soccer practice. The hardest, most skill-driven drills can be saved for the end of a workout so the coach can highlight how fatigue produces fear-driven results. A basketball coach can use dummy bags against players facing a defender in the low post.

In all of these scenarios, we see that circumstances are causing the athletes to second guess their actions and start making mistakes. This causes even more fatigue and things go from bad to worse. Most athletes tend to avoid being physically fatigued because of the pain.

It's not just fatigue that causes fear. Pride is also a big factor. Pride can cause athletes to have the fear of failure, the fear of looking bad or the fear or letting people down. No matter the root cause of fear, players must be willing to deal with it if they want to take their game to the next level.

After those practice drills and film sessions, I've often had athletes come to me admitting their fear. That's exactly what you want. Their transparency and vulnerability is key. Now we can deal with the problem. Now we can give them the antidote to that fear.

FROM FEAR TO FAITH

In the New Testament, the disciples likewise had moments where their fear was exposed, but none more trying than in the hours leading up to Jesus' death. Here's the interesting thing. Jesus had been trying to tell them what was on the horizon for a while. Each time, however, they failed to make the connection.

"The Son of Man is going to be delivered into the hands of men. They will kill him, and after three days he will rise." But they did not understand what he meant and were afraid to ask him about it. (Mark 9:31-32)

In another instance, Peter actually rebuked Jesus for suggesting He was going to die. As you can imagine, that didn't go well for Peter.

But when Jesus turned and looked at his disciples, he rebuked Peter. "Get behind me, Satan!" he said. "You do not have in mind the concerns of God, but merely human concerns." (Mark 8:33)

So when the time came for Jesus to be arrested and tried, the disciples were predictably afraid and scurried in every direction. Ironically, Peter, the one who boldly claimed he would die for Jesus (Matthew 26:35), denied knowing Him three times to strangers in the crowd (Luke 22:54-62).

As Jesus was brutally tortured and then nailed to the cross, only the disciple John remained and stayed to the very end to comfort Mary as she and a few other women mourned. Then, for three days, the disciples hid in fear that the Roman soldiers would come for them too. Imagine their surprise when Jesus, very much alive, miraculously appeared and forgave them for their fear and disbelief.

Those same disciples later became powerful ambassadors of the gospel known as apostles, even under great duress and persecution. What was different? This time they had the power of the Holy Spirit that gave them courage to move from fear to faith. They were strong in spirit and wouldn't let any circumstances keep them from completing the mission.

THE CIRCUMSTANCE-FREE LIFE

In sports and in life, there are two ways to live, circumstance-based or circumstance-free. If you're circumstance-based, you're always reacting to what's going on around you or to what you think is going to happen. It's a life dictated by fear. On the other hand, if you're circumstance-free, you're not concerned about what's going to happen or worried about the outcome. It's a life of freedom.

Athletes need to know that Jesus Christ is the only antidote to their fear. They might not accept it, but they should at least have the opportunity to think about it and consider it. They need to know they can't overcome fear by simply mustering up the courage from within, pulling up their bootstraps or listening to motivational speakers. Those things might help for a while, but they just take away the symptom. They don't bring healing.

At the same time, however, fear isn't something that Jesus can just zap away. There are some steps we have to take in order to enjoy the freedom of the circumstance-free life.

1) Identify the fear. You can't address the problem if you don't know the specific nature of the problem. This requires honest reflection, counsel from mature Christians, and an open line of communication with the Holy Spirit.

Have nothing to do with the fruitless deeds of darkness, but rather expose them. (Ephesians 5:11)

A wise coach will implement drills that expose their athlete's weakness and create circumstances for them to grow in their sport and faith.

2) Repent of fear. Living in fear is a sin, but thank God, we have a remedy. It's the death and resurrection of our Lord. You may have fear all around you, but you don't have to live in that fear. You can take your first steps toward conquering fear by asking the Lord to forgive you of that sin and then turning away from it. When you repent, you aren't just rejecting fear. More importantly, you are accepting Jesus' perfect love.

There is no fear in love. But perfect love drives out fear, because fear has to do with punishment. The one who fears is not made perfect in love. (1 John 4:18)

3) Eliminate pride. Fear is almost always based on pride. Pride will cause you to worry about what others think or be afraid of failure. That's why you must fight against pride daily. Otherwise, you'll never be able to conquer fear.

So put away all pride from yourselves. You are standing under the powerful hand of God. At the right time He will lift you up. Give all your worries to Him because He cares for you. (1 Peter 5:6-7)

4) Retrain your brain. Our victory comes from an inside-out, personal relationship with Jesus. We have to be trained in the scriptures. We have to be in tune with the Holy Spirit who gives us the power through that training to tackle all situations.

For the Spirit God gave us does not make us timid, but gives us power, love and self-discipline. (2 Timothy 1:7)

5) Pray for courage. Any time you're facing a particular fear, turn it into a prayer. When you openly communicate with the Lord about your fear, the power of Christ will come through you and start to weed it out of your life. That means you might need to confess in the middle of a game or in the middle of a play and proclaim you are trusting God in that moment. It can be something as simple as, "Lord, there's fear all around me, but I'm focusing on you. I'm concentrating on you."

"I have told you these things, so that in me you may have peace. In this world you will have trouble. But take heart! I have overcome the world." (John 16:33)

When you're living the circumstance-free life, you can have the courage to act fearlessly in the midst of fear. When fear is swirling all around you, you can bravely stand for integrity by bringing your best and not allowing people, pressures or worries to dictate your actions.

Overcoming fear doesn't mean you won't get hit. It means you can endure the hit. You can endure whatever comes your way with Jesus. Then, you will show the world what it means to live with courage. Focus on Jesus during your most fearful times, and He will respond with the promises from God's Word.

STUDY QUESTIONS

1. Describe some situations where you've found yourself fearful during athletic training or competition. How have you typically dealt with that fear?

2. When have you found yourself fearful during life in general? How have you typically dealt with that fear?

3. Why do you think the disciples struggled with fear even though they were walking alongside Jesus?

4. Think about times when you are most afraid. What do you think might be the root cause of that fear?

5. Go back and look at the five ways you can live a circumstance-free life. What are some specific steps you can start taking today that will help you begin to conquer your fear?

6

CHAPTER SIX

~~~~~~~~

YARDS
AFTER CATCH

A Parable About Determination

> # "Some people want it to happen. Some wish it would happen. Others make it happen." – Michael Jordan

Can you imagine if the NFL had a rule where you had to stop at the point of the catch? What if the NBA didn't allow players to dribble, but instead they could only pass to advance the ball? Would there be any excitement in Major League Baseball if they did away with extra base hits?

It's the added effort that brings so much intrigue and excitement to the games we play. Determination to make something happen and keep a play alive is what compels fans to come back for more.

It's that x-factor that makes us appreciate superstars like basketball legend Michael Jordan. The six-time NBA champion, five-time league MVP and oft-labeled "greatest of all time" once made a powerful statement about the contrast between those who have determination and those who don't.

"Some people want it to happen. Some wish it would happen. Others make it happen."

The same is true in life. The desire to be better, do better and help others to be better is a powerful fuel that humans need to fill up on every day. It's what gets us out of bed and gives us the drive to make a difference.

YARDS AFTER CATCH

In football a lot can happen after a completed pass, and even though the quarterback gets credits for all the yardage, it's often the receivers, tight ends, and running backs who end up doing a lot of the work.

Any advancement of the ball after the reception is referred to as YAC or yards after catch. It's the ability to do something with the ball after you've caught it. During the 2018 NFL season, there were 61,710 yards gained after catches, which accounted for 49 percent of all receiving yards.

These plays are often some of the most exciting moments in a game. Receivers juke to avoid getting tackled. They make sharp cuts to get a quicker angle to the end zone. Running backs who receive short passes out of the backfield churn their legs and fight through defenders to gain every last inch of territory.

Yards after a catch don't just happen because of pure athletic ability. It also requires great skill, refined technique and innate instinct. The receiver has to keep his eyes wide open and know where he's going. He has to know when to cut back against the grain or when to make a dip move and then explode back to the outside. He has to be adept at using his free arm as the lead block and an explosive tool to keep defenders off his body. When you blend those elements with sheer determination, progress is made and great things happen.

MARCH ON

The Book of Exodus tells the epic story of how God used Moses to free the Israelites from Egyptian captivity. That led God's people on a journey to the Promised Land, but it was anything but easy. In fact, the Israelites went through great adversity and faced many obstacles along the way.

In Numbers 13 and 14, the Israelites had finally arrived in Canaan. Moses commissioned 12 spies to survey the land and its people. Of the 10 spies, only two, Joshua and Caleb, came back with a good report. The land was fruitful and plenteous. It was ripe for the conquest. The others, however, came back scared. There were giants in the land. There was no way they could win the battle.

The people listened to the 10 spies and gave up hope. There was no reason to continue. There was nothing left to fight for. They had been saved from Egyptian captivity and were now content to stop short of the goal.

This angered God. He proclaimed the Israelites would wander for another 40 years before going to the Promised Land, and anyone over the age of 20 would not be allowed in—all except Joshua and Caleb.

Those 40 years passed, and the Israelites found themselves back in Canaan. By now, Moses had died and God had placed Joshua in charge. This time was different than before. The Israelites were hungry for victory. They were full of determination and fight.

In Joshua 6, the people were encamped outside Jericho. The city's towering walls were secure and impenetrable. Joshua went to hear from the Lord and came back with an unusual plan.

Then the LORD said to Joshua, "See, I have delivered Jericho into your hands, along with its king and its fighting men. March around the city once with all the armed men. Do this for six days. Have seven priests carry trumpets of rams' horns in front of the ark. On the seventh day, march around the city seven times, with the priests blowing the trumpets. When you hear them sound a long blast on the trumpets, have the whole army give a loud shout; then the wall of the city will collapse and the army will go up, everyone straight in." (Joshua 6:2-5)

Joshua could have looked at the situation much like the 10 spies did 40 years earlier. He could have dropped the ball and walked away from the field of play. Instead, he obeyed God and followed through with great determination.

After six grueling days, Joshua didn't give up. The next morning, he gathered the priests and the army one more time and led the people to victory as the trumpets sounded and the walls crumbled down.

FIGHT ON

Sometimes in life you just have to keep moving. There are moments when you want to throw in the towel and give up, but those are the moments when victory is right around the corner. The winning score is just a few yards away.

When we receive Jesus Christ as our Lord and Savior, we're called to advance the gospel as far as we can go. We get numerous opportunities to share the gospel. There are going to be times that we get tackled. There's going to be persecution. It's going to be tough.

That's when we rely on the spiritual techniques we've been given: studying the word of God, being prayerful, connecting with others, taking advantage of the protections we've been given.

Sometimes God decides He wants to do something big. It's an amazing answer to prayer. It's miraculous. It's incredible. It's like an 80-yard bomb. Most of the time, however, we're making short strides in life. It's not always that spectacular. Other times we're gaining a little ground at a time and God is expecting us to make something of it, like that proverbial lateral pass you have to fight to turn into a 30-yard gain.

That's what the life of spiritual determination is about. That's what it means to fight on and make something happen. Here are a few ways to advance the gospel and do more through the determined life.

1. Be Kingdom-minded. See the big picture. Understand that the small things add up. Your daily effort may not always feel effective, but when you trust God, He can turn those incremental gains into long-term impact.

To the faithful you show yourself faithful. (Psalm 18:25a)

2. Be prepared. Have a line of attack against the enemy. Memorize scripture. Take authority over him and rebuke him when he tries to stop you from moving forward.

Be alert and of sober mind. Your enemy the devil prowls around like a roaring lion looking for someone to devour. (1 Peter 5:8)

3. Be grateful. Be thankful for the little victories. Don't complain about the setbacks.

Give thanks in all circumstances; for this is God's will for you in Christ Jesus. (1 Thessalonians 5:18)

4. Be a fighter. Jesus didn't give up when He was suffering on the cross for your sins. Don't give up on Him. Don't give up on yourself. Don't give up on the lost family members and friends who need you to reach them with the gospel.

Let us not become weary in doing good, for at the proper time we will reap a harvest if we do not give up. (Galatians 6:9)

STUDY QUESTIONS

1. What does it mean to give extra effort in your sport? How is determination and drive usually rewarded?

2. Why do you think the Israelites gave up on the goal (The Promised Land) at the first sign of difficulty? Why do you think they were more determined the second time around?

3. Describe a time when you were tempted to give up short of your goal. What did you do and what were the results of your decision?

4. What are some circumstances in your life when your determination and drive are low? Conversely, what are some times when you feel like you have great determination and drive?

5. What are areas in your life where you could use more determination?

7

CHAPTER SEVEN

~~~~~~~~~~

FOCAL POINTS

A Parable About Focus

> **"Let your eyes look straight ahead; fix your gaze directly before you."**
> **– King Solomon**

King Solomon was one of Israel's most successful leaders. During his 40-year reign, he ushered in an era of peace and prosperity and famously built the first Holy Temple in Jerusalem.

Solomon's success was the direct result of his great wisdom, and 1 Kings 3:3-15 tells us that his wisdom came directly from God. Many of his sage musings can be found in the Song of Solomon, the Ecclesiastes and the Book of Proverbs, where he talks about topics such as generosity, hard work, self-control, and focus.

Sometimes, however, Solomon struggled to follow his own advice, especially in the areas of self-control and focus. As time passed, he grew increasingly distracted by the three F's: fame, fortune and females.

That last item on the list was particularly problematic. Solomon's household grew to include 700 wives and 300 other women who were simply there to provide physical pleasure. He knew what was right, yet he lost focus on what God had commanded him to do. Many of the women he invited into his palace brought with them false gods, which led Solomon even further astray. Eventually, he saw his great nation decline until it was split apart under the leadership of his son Rehoboam.

In other words, Solomon's lack of focus turned what should have been a legacy of glorious victory into a cautionary tale of shame and defeat.

PINK ELEPHANTS, BLUE MONKEYS

No matter the sport, focus is one of the most important characteristics any athlete can have. Great talent is diluted, if not completely meaningless, without it.

When coaching receivers, I taught my players different techniques to stay focused on the ball as it leaves the quarterback's hands and spirals towards them. For instance, I would tell them to focus on a smaller portion or simply get their nose lined up to the point of the ball.

Beyond the technical aspects of focus, there are also times athletes need to be reminded of the importance of staying focused emotionally, not allowing distractions like what's going on in the stands or who is watching at home to take them off their game.

For my athletes who were believers, I often took the concept to the next level and talked to them about staying focused spiritually no matter the situation, whether that might be in the classroom, in their relationships, on the practice field or on the field of competition.

One of my favorite examples is former Nebraska running back Roy Helu Jr. Roy didn't live or die by football. He was a down-to-earth, fun-loving guy who never took himself too seriously. He had a humble simplicity and was very coachable.

During the 2010 season, Roy set a school record against Missouri with 307 yards rushing. It was also the top national performance that week, and he was getting a lot of attention both locally and across the country. Roy came to me a few days later with a dilemma.

"Coach, I'm having a hard time focusing on the Lord," he said. "I want to give Him the glory but my mind keeps drifting back to me. How can I get my mind off myself?"

"If I tell you to not think about pink elephants, what are you going to think about?" I asked.

"Pink elephants," he replied.

"So what can you think about to keep you from thinking about pink elephants?"

Roy thought about it for about five seconds and then gave a response like only he could.

"Blue monkeys!"

After enjoying a nice laugh, I made one final point that he later told me lingered throughout the rest of his college career and then in the NFL.

"Get your mind on Christ and it won't be on you."

FOCAL POINTS

So what does it look like to fix our eyes on Jesus, and can it really be done in a meaningful, sustainable way through athletic competition?

The answer is a resounding "Yes!" For the athlete, the principle of spiritual focus can be practiced in many different ways. Consistently keeping one's mind on Christ isn't easy, but it can be attained with something Wes Neal, author of **The Handbook on Athletic Perfection**, refers to as focal points—reminders to worship the Lord and give Him the glory in all things.

Here's an example:

On November 25, 2011, it was the day after Thanksgiving and Nebraska was about to play Iowa at Memorial Stadium in Lincoln. Nearly 76,000 fans were pouring in to cheer on the Huskers.

During pregame warm-ups, I struck up a conversation with our star running back Rex Burkhead, who was a follower of Christ.

"Look up at that crowd, Rex," I said. "They're here to see you run the ball. Who are you playing for today?"

"I'm here to play for the glory of Christ," he responded.

"That's right," I said. "You're going to run like a wild animal if you'll just let Christ take control of your life and if you'll run for His glory. How are you going to remember that during the game?"

Rex was perplexed. He thought about it for a minute but couldn't come up with a response.

"Look up at those goal posts," I interjected. "What do they remind you of?"

Rex again took a moment to ponder the question before answering.

"It kind of looks like a cross," he finally replied.

"That's right, Rex," I affirmed. "And you have one in both end zone. No matter which direction you're running, you use those goal posts as a focal point to remind you that Jesus died on the cross for your sin. He paid a dear price for it. He was resurrected from the dead, and He offered you eternal life. You accepted that eternal life, and now your life has changed forever. Wouldn't it be a great way to thank Him and give Him glory be to run with reckless abandon with Him in mind as a worship offering?"

Rex never forgot that conversation and continued to use the goal posts as a focal point throughout the rest of his career. Oh, and during that game, he did run wild for 163 yards and a touchdown, plus a school record 38 carries!

So what are some other focal points an athlete might use?

Another good one for football can be found on the actual game ball. Looking at the pigskin, its stitches run horizontally and vertically and form the shape of a cross.

Athletes can write Bible verses or draw crosses on their wristbands, batting gloves, ball caps, hockey sticks, golf balls, cleats, skates or shoes.

A soccer player might look at the open goal and think about the empty tomb. A baseball player might look down at home plate during an at bat and be reminded of the heavenly home that awaits us.

Or you can come up with your own focal point specific to your sport and unique to your personality. No matter what you use, all of these things can all serve as constant reminders to worship God during training, practice and competition.

STUDY QUESTIONS

1. On a scale of 1-10, how would you rate your overall focus (1 being extremely unfocused, 10 being highly focused)?

2. What are some areas in which you have less focus? What about some areas in which you have more focus? Can you explain why?

3. What are the most prominent things on your mind during competition? Do you find it easy or difficult to think about Christ or think about giving God glory?

4. How do you think having a Kingdom mindset (focusing on His glory) might impact the way you compete?

5. What are some focal points you can start using to help keep your mind on Christ during competition?

8

~~~~~

CHAPTER EIGHT

THE HOUND AND THE HARE

A Parable About Motivation

> # "It makes a difference when you treat every day like the Super Bowl."
> ## – Rex Burkhead

Motivation is one of the most important characteristics in sports. It can be an athlete's best friend or worst enemy. Motivation can determine a team's success or failure. It can make the difference between reaching the finish line and giving up before the race is won.

When talking to my players, I often use one of Aesop's fables to challenge them in the area of motivation. In the story, a hound sniffs out a hare and forces it out of his home. The hare darts and dodges as the hound gives chase. Eventually however, the hound gets tired and the hare uses one last burst of energy to escape.

In the distance, a herd of goats that has been watching the scene unfold begins to mock the hound for allowing the hare to best him. Before finishing the fable, I then ask the players a question, "Why do you think the hound failed to catch the hare?"

"The hound was having a bad day," one player responds. "He didn't get much sleep."

"Maybe the terrain was wet," another responds.

"The hound needed more agility training," an especially astute athlete opines.

Most of their answers usually relate back to their plight on the football field but miss the simplistic message Aesop was trying to convey.

"You do not see the difference between us," the hound replied to the goats. *"I was only running for dinner, but he for his life."*

THE MOST IMPORTANT DAYS

Rex Burkhead is one of my former athletes at Nebraska. Although he was an undersized running back, he went on to become a successful NFL player with a Super Bowl ring to show for his efforts. Rex won that championship with the New England Patriots in 2019. I once asked him what made the Patriots such a successful organization.

"It makes a difference when you treat every day like the Super Bowl," he said.

His simple but powerful response brings me back to "The Hound and the Hare." When I shared that fable with my players, it was an opportunity to talk about things like motivation, desire and drive. They needed to take honest stock of what was going on deep inside their hearts.

It really does matter because being an athlete can be a grind. Football players, for instance, have one game each week, usually on Saturday or Sunday. It can become easy to get stuck in the routine. Instead of remembering why they are lifting weights, going to practice, and eating right, he can lose sight of the big picture.

If he's not careful, he won't be able to see far enough ahead. He'll lose his passion. He'll forget that game day is right around the corner and everything he does now is going to affect what he does on the field of competition. The most important days are Tuesday, Wednesday and Thursday

Like that hound, however, all he's thinking about is the next moment. There's no desire to give your best effort when the motivation to succeed on game day has been suppressed. There's no need to fight when there's no sense of urgency.

LIVING WATER

Jesus was always motivated. He wasn't fighting for His own life, but rather fighting for the lives of others. His desire to reach lost and hurting people often caused Him to squelch His physical needs.

Take for example the story found in John 4 where Jesus met a Samaritan woman who was drawing water from a well. There were two interesting things about this particular scenario.

First of all, the disciples were nowhere to be found. They had left Jesus in search of food. They were tired and hungry from their recent journey. Helping more people was the last thing on their minds.

Secondly, Jesus was breaking societal norms in order to interact with this woman. Jews typically saw themselves as better than Samaritans, and men didn't typically interact with women in public. Jesus, however, had a much higher purpose and had no problem going against the grain to accomplish His mission.

Here's how that conversation went.

When a Samaritan woman came to draw water, Jesus said to her, "Will you give me a drink?" (v. 7)

The Samaritan woman said to him, "You are a Jew, and I am a Samaritan woman. How can you ask me for a drink?" (For Jews do not associate with Samaritans.)

Jesus answered her, "If you knew the gift of God and who it is that asks you for a drink, you would have asked him and he would have given you living water."

"Sir," the woman said, "you have nothing to draw with and the well is deep. Where can you get this living water? Are you greater than our father Jacob, who gave us the well and drank from it himself, as did also his sons and his livestock?"

Jesus answered, "Everyone who drinks this water will be thirsty again, but whoever drinks the water I give them will never thirst. Indeed, the water I give them will become in them a spring of water welling up to eternal life." (vv. 9-14)

Certainly Jesus was hungry and thirsty just like the disciples, but at that moment He wasn't concerned with his physical body. This woman had a thirsty spirit and a hungry heart. Because of that, Jesus focused on the bigger prize. He put aside His needs in order to give her something much more valuable than food or water. He was fighting for her salvation. Jesus was fighting to give her eternal life.

WHAT'S YOUR MOTIVATION?

In "The Hound and the Hare," there were two very different motivations. The hound's hunger for lunch couldn't match the hare's hunger to stay alive. In the story of Jesus and the woman at the well, Jesus' hunger to deliver the life-saving gospel to the woman was far greater than His physical hunger for food and water.

What is it for you? What's your motivation? Do you have a deep hunger to get closer to God? Do you have a sense of urgency to reach the world for Christ? At the end of the day, it's the priority of your life that will govern what you will fight for and how hard you will fight for it.

If you see a person who's not all that excited about spiritual things or about the scriptures, it's probably because he or she is running for lunch, not running for their life. A lunch date doesn't compare to a life mate! When it's life or death, there's going to be passion and drive even when it gets tough.

If you invest in your relationship with Jesus, the Lord will reward you and give you the enthusiasm and strength to work through hunger and fatigue. He'll keep pouring His strength back into you.

Whether it's your spiritual walk or your call to reach the lost, priorities drive motivation and motivation drives passion. At some point, you have to realize that the stakes are high.

Your relationship with God should be the most important thing in your life. Your ability to fulfill His purpose for your life depends on it. On the other hand, your call to reach the lost is the most important thing you can do with your life. Someone else's life depends on it.

STUDY QUESTIONS

1. In "The Hound and the Hare," which character most resembles you? Explain.

2. What do you think it means to be spiritually hungry?

3. On a scale of 1-10 (1 being "no appetite," 10 being "starving") how would you currently rate your hunger to get closer to God? What about your desire to reach the lost?

4. What are some things that might be keeping you from having a sense of urgency for your spiritual growth and sharing the gospel?

5. What steps can you take today that might help you become more motivated to get closer to God and fulfill your calling to reach the lost?

9

CHAPTER NINE

GOOD ON PAPER

A Parable About The Heart

"The thing you can't measure is someone's heart." – Shannon Sharpe

Every year, executives from all the major professional sports leagues have the exciting yet unenviable job of drafting athletes to play for their teams. They spend hundreds of hours breaking down film, scouting live action, constructing selection board, and hoping against hope that everything works out in their favor.

Sometimes it does. Sometimes it doesn't. That's because it's impossible to know how an athlete will perform until they've been thrown into real game scenarios.

Take for instance Shannon Sharpe, who was a little known NCAA Division II tight end from Savannah State. He wasn't highly recruited out of high school but shone brightly enough to get the NFL's attention. It didn't hurt that his older brother Sterling Sharpe was already lighting it up with the Green Bay Packers. Still, no one wanted to risk a premium pick on an unproven D2 player.

At the 1990 NFL Draft, Sharpe fell all the way to the seventh round where the Denver Broncos finally gave him a shot. It turned out to be the steal of the draft. In 14 seasons, Sharpe helped the Broncos win three Super Bowls, was selected to play in eight Pro Bowls and was inducted into the Pro Football Hall of Fame

Ten years later, a more well known quarterback from the University of Michigan was the 199th pick in the sixth round of the 2000 NFL Draft. Nearly two decades later, 31 teams not named the New England Patriots who are still trying to figure out how they missed on Tom Brady, six-time Super Bowl champion, four-time Super Bowl MVP, three-time NFL MVP and 14-time Pro Bowl selection.

Miscues are endless and cross over into all professional sports. In the 2007 NBA Draft, the Portland Trailblazers used its top pick to select Greg Oden over Kevin Durant, who went onto become an NBA MVP and two-time NBA champion.

A few years earlier, at the 1998 NBA Draft, the Los Angeles Clippers passed up the likes of Vince Carter, Dirk Nowitzki and Paul Pierce to take Michael Olowokandi with the number one selection.

No matter how you break it down, it all goes to show you can't always judge future success by just looking at physical or statistical measurables. Like Shannon Sharpe once aptly said, "The thing you can't measure is someone's heart."

STAR GAZING

After the 2011 season, a junior defensive end from Wisconsin named J.J. Watt declared for the NFL Draft. That next season was Nebraska's first as a member of the Big 10. In other words, we missed facing up against the dominant All-American by one year.

Watt's rise to stardom was unconventional. He was a two-star recruit with a lone NCAA FBS scholarship offer from Central Michigan. After head coach Butch Jones suggested he switch from tight end to offensive tackle, Watt decided to walk on at Wisconsin, where he converted to defensive end.

His gutsy decision paid off. Two years later he was the 11th overall pick in the 2011 NFL Draft and has been one of the league's top pass rushers ever since. After someone on social media poked fun at his lightly regarded high school career, Watt responded with a quip that likewise poked fun at the very imperfect recruiting system.

"You keep your five stars. I'll keep my two," Watt wrote. "And the two Defensive Player of the Year trophies that match."

To be fair, evaluating talent is one of a coach's toughest jobs, especially college programs looking at high school athletes. There are the obvious things to evaluate like speed, agility, quickness, explosiveness, physical stature and intelligence, but what about intangibles like character, dedication, determination, respectfulness, toughness and heart.

Then you have to go even deeper and ask the hard questions. What happens when they get tired? Do they play with fear? Are they lazy? Are they greedy? Are they selfish? Those things can be difficult to evaluate from a distance and sometimes aren't discovered until it's too late.

When you do discover those issues while recruiting, there are times you have to make a tough decision. You might have to go with the less talented player who has better character. In the long run, you're going to be better off with that kid rather than the athlete who has all the talent in the world but lacks those key intangibles. No question.

Fans get caught up in star-gazing, but these are the things that really matter. Coaches have to resist the temptation to look at predetermined rankings that many times turn out to be incorrect. Time and again it's been proven that many players are overrated while others are underestimated. A player might look good on paper, but that five-star rating won't mean anything if they're not good on the field or, more importantly, good on the inside.

THE HEART TEST

For the better part of 400 years, Israel operated without traditional leadership. Instead, judges and prophets served as God's liaisons to the people. Over time, the Israelites grew discontented with this arrangement. They looked across the region and coveted what the surrounding nations had that they didn't—a king.

The leading prophet at the time was a man named Samuel. God

tasked him with finding and anointing Israel's first king. His name was Saul, and he was a great warrior in the Israelite army. You might say he was a five-star recruit.

Saul looked the part. He was strong, skilled, intelligent and handsome. He was good on paper. Saul also had flaws. He was prideful, impatient, petulant and jealous. He lacked some important intangibles necessary to lead successfully.

King Saul started strong, however, and was wise to listen to God's instructions. He had a good relationship with Samuel as well. This helped Saul maintain Israel's status as a dominant nation.

Then, things started to go in a bad direction. On several occasions, Saul sinned against God through acts of disobedience such as burning an offering to God himself (1 Samuel 13) and sparing the life of an enemy king and taking spoils of war that were supposed to be destroyed (1 Samuel 15).

This angered God. It was time to start looking for Saul's replacement.

Again, Samuel was called upon to lead the search. The Lord sent him to the town of Bethlehem, where he would find the new king in the house of Jesse.

When Samuel saw Jesse's oldest son Eliab, he was convinced this must be the young man who would take Saul's place, but God had something else in mind.

"Do not consider his appearance or his height, for I have rejected him. The Lord does not look at the things people look at. People look at the outward appearance, but the Lord looks at the heart." (1 Samuel 16:7)

Samuel looked at Jesse's next oldest son, Abinadab. He wasn't the one. Then he observed the next oldest son, Shammah. He wasn't the one, either. Seven sons passed by Samuel and none of them were the one. They all looked the part. They all looked like five-star recruits, but the Lord was looking for something deeper than physical stature.

There had to be someone else.

Jesse had one more son named David who was tending the sheep. He was just a young teenage boy. No recruiting services had noticed him yet. No one was scouting him in the meadow. Yet when Samuel saw him, he instantly knew that God had chosen David to be anointed king.

Everyone else missed the mark. They didn't see what God saw. They hadn't seen the boy with the warrior's heart. They hadn't witnessed his courage as he bravely killed a lion and a bear in order to protect his sheep. They hadn't listened to him sing original psalms of praise and worship to the Lord. They looked at David's outward appearance, but God looked his heart.

The world would eventually see what God had seen. David famously stepped up to defeat Goliath, the Philistine giant, as King Saul and his mighty army cowered in fear. As he grew into manhood, David's fame continued to grow to the point where an envious and enraged Saul tried to have him killed.

Saul's story didn't end well. On the verge of a massive military defeat, he fell on his sword to avoid capture. His tragic death ushered in David as the new king. Even though David also made mistakes, he always came back to God and set himself and the nation of Israel on a righteous path.

Hundreds of years later, the apostle Paul recounted David's unlikely rise to fame in a sermon and quoted God's words from the Old Testament scriptures.

"I have found David son of Jesse, a man after my own heart; he will do everything I want him to do." (1 Samuel 13:14, Acts 13:22)

In the beginning, David might not have looked good on paper, but the story of his life has lived on for thousands of years because he had intangibles that couldn't be measured.

TRUE VALUE

We can get caught star-gazing sometimes. We live in a world that places far too much value on physical appearance, talent and success. Too often we think those attributes make up the barometer that decides who God can use, but sometimes people with those outward attributes don't have the right heart to serve God.

Conversely, David was one of many Bible heroes who didn't necessarily look the part. Joseph was a bragger. Samson was a womanizer. Moses was a stutterer. Rahab was a prostitute. Ruth was a widow. Nehemiah was a cupbearer. Peter was a hot head. Yet they all did great things for God.

That's great news for us. We don't have to look good on paper. We each have special callings on our lives, and God has equipped us with the specific gifts and talents that we need to fulfill His purpose. Ultimately, your true value to Him isn't your appearance or your talent, but rather what's inside your heart.

I praise you because I am fearfully and wonderfully made; your works are wonderful, I know that full well. (Psalm 139:14)

You might feel like you're inadequate because you don't check all the boxes, but God can use anyone if they are surrendered to Him and are willing to obey His commands and walk boldly in His name.

As we do that, we also need to stop assigning stars and ranking people by their abilities and appearance. It's time to follow God's lead, stop looking at the outward man and start looking inward at the heart.

STUDY QUESTIONS

1. If you were recruiting or scouting athletes, what physical attributes would be most important to you? Which intangibles would you be looking for?

2. What about Saul made him an attractive king to the Israelites? Why do you think David wasn't an obvious choice to replace Saul?

3. Describe a time when you didn't feel like you had the right attributes or abilities to be successful as a competitor on the field or as a contributor in life. How did comparison to others play into your mindset and what, if anything, did you do to address those struggles?

4. What inspiration might you draw from David's story or from the stories of other Bible heroes who did great things for God in spite of their imperfections?

5. What are some things you can start doing today that will help you see your true value to God?

10

CHAPTER TEN

~~~~~~~~

THE
LOCKER ROOM

A Parable About The Kingdom of Heaven

"Sports is something that transcends generations, transcends backgrounds, cultures, races." – Malcolm Jenkins

Throughout the history of the United States, there have been times when we have found ourselves divided over things like politics, religion, war, social issues and race.

The sports locker room, however, has been a place where many of the walls we sometimes erect are broken down.

Recently, for instance, we've seen an uptick in racial tensions tied to complex issues such as poverty, housing, law enforcement, criminal justice, border security and the National Anthem. Athletes have become more vocal about their personal stances and solutions to these problems.

Even though there are differences of opinion, their contributions to these debates have brought much needed attention and clarity. At the end of the day the locker room has provided great examples of unity throughout even the most tumultuous of times. Malcolm Jenkins, Philadelphia Eagles cornerback, social justice advocate and follower of Christ, made this astute observation.

"Sports is something that transcends generations, transcends backgrounds, cultures, races."

This has certainly been the case as our nation has made strides toward racial equality in particular thanks to the barrier breaking contributions of great athletes like Jackie Robinson, Satchell Paige, Fitz Pollard, Earl Lloyd, Jesse Owens, Althea Gibson, Wilma Rudolph, Venus and Serena Williams, and Tiger Woods.

This beautiful tapestry is becoming more diversified all the time with athletes coming from all over the globe to take part in the American sports experience. That's what makes the locker room such a special place.

THE LOCKER ROOM

Throughout my 40-plus years as a coach, I've been blessed to be around a rich diversity of players. Our teams have included young men from rural areas and cities. There have been white guys, black guys and many other ethnic groups represented. We've had players with all kinds of political persuasions, socio-economic backgrounds and religious beliefs.

Something happened during my first stint at Nebraska that helped me see the potential within the locker room even more. At the time, I was an assistant coach under the legendary Tom Osborne. We finished the 1990 season with two embarrassing losses. Injuries were a factor, but Coach Osborne felt like something else deserved part of the blame. Our team wasn't unified.

Coach Osborne spoke to Jack Stark, a psychologist from Omaha, who suggested that the team form something he called the Unity Council. This group would be comprised of players selected by their teammates and would include two members of each group (two running backs, two receivers, two defensive linemen, etc.).

The Unity Council met once a week. The only staff member in the room was Boyd Epley, our strength coach, whose job was to bring any concerns to Coach Osborne on the players' behalf. Some of the issues were minor. Some were pretty big. In all cases, Coach Osborne was judicious and fair and used the opportunity to give the team a voice.

Over time, we started to see a difference. Players started to get a sense that they were all being treated equally and fairly, from the starting lineup down to the walk-ons. Team morale improved as everyone worked together to complete important tasks such as vision casting, goal setting and even helping Coach Osborne create disciplinary rules and consequences.

In Coach Osborne's final five seasons, the team's incredible run included a 60-3 record, three undefeated teams and three national championships in 1994, 1995 and 1997. Sure we had good talent, experienced coaches, ample resources, supportive administrators and one of the most consistent fan bases in the country. Internally, however, we knew that the Unity Council played a big part in strengthening the locker room and preparing our athletes for the task at hand.

A MASTERPIECE OF MISFITS

When Jesus recruited 12 disciples to follow Him, He intentionally picked people who came from different backgrounds, professions and personalities.

For instance, Peter, Andrew, James and John were all fishermen but had varying attributes. Peter was known for his brash boldness. John, on the other hand, was known for his fierce loyalty. Andrew had great enthusiasm, and James displayed notable business acumen.

Matthew was a tax collector and probably not very popular amongst the people thanks to the bad reputation that often accompanied his profession.

Thomas was a religious zealot whose courageous loyalty was shockingly replaced with cynicism and doubt following Christ's crucifixion.

Simon was believed to be a political activist who became known for his passion to follow and serve Jesus.

Others within the inner circle were equally diverse. There were average men like Thaddeus, Matthias and Barnabas. There were also several women who followed and supported Jesus' ministry, an unlikely cast of characters that included: Mary Magdalene, a demon-possessed prostitute Jesus delivered; Joanna, the wife of Herod's steward; Mary, the mother of James and John; and a woman named Susanna.

After Jesus ascended into heaven, His followers grew in numbers and the disciples became great leaders within the Early Church known as apostles. God's team not only got bigger. It got more diverse.

The apostle Paul was unique due to his devout Jewish upbringing as a Roman citizen. Luke the evangelist was a Greek physician who wrote nearly a quarter of the New Testament (the Gospel of Luke and the Acts of the Apostles). There were young men like Timothy, who had both Jewish and Greek heritage, along with his mother Eunice and grandmother Lois.

It was a masterpiece of misfits, divinely brought together as a unified group that would change the world forever. They certainly didn't agree on everything all the time, but in the end, most of them would give their lives for the sake of Christ and the advancement of the gospel.

THE KINGDOM OF HEAVEN

The locker room is a great analogy for the Kingdom of Heaven. It was likewise demonstrated in the way Jesus chose His disciples and empowered the apostles.

Today, if we are going to fulfill the Great Commission (Matthew 28:16-20) and win the lost for Him, we will have to get past our petty differences, come together and be unified. That means breaking down socio-economic, racial and political barriers.

God doesn't have a race or a people group other than those who have trusted in Jesus as their Lord and Savior. In fact, there's a beautiful portrayal of the Kingdom of Heaven that the apostle John saw through a divine vision.

"After this I looked, and there before me was a great multitude that no one could count, from every nation, tribe, people and language, standing before the throne and before the Lamb. They were wearing white robes and were holding palm branches in their hands." (Revelation 7:9)

Even though we have issues of division in our society, we as believers shouldn't see each other that way. We need to do things differently.

Can we be intentional about our fellow brothers and sisters in Christ? Can we go to other parts of town and experience life with believers who live differently than us? Can we be ambassadors and examples of what the Kingdom of Heaven looks like?

As believers, we are great witnesses for Jesus when we come together as people from different backgrounds and unite as one. The lost will covet the relationships we have with each other. They will see our unity and want to be a part of His holy church.

"By this everyone will know that you are my disciples, if you love one another." (John 13:35)

It doesn't stop there. We also need to be unified in our message. We have to be willing to rightly divide the truth. Unity isn't about getting large numbers of people together. Unity is a crystallization of the truth with likeminded people. That means coming together in one accord and taking Paul's timely advice.

I appeal to you, brothers and sisters, in the name of our Lord Jesus Christ, that all of you agree with one another in what you say and that there be no divisions among you, but that you be perfectly united in mind and thought. (1 Corinthians 1:10)

Years earlier, Jesus also shared His desire for unity within the Church through a powerful prayer.

"I have given them the glory that you gave me, that they may be one as we are one—I in them and you in me—so that they may be

brought to complete unity. Then the world will know that you sent me and have loved them even as you have loved me." (John 17:22-23)

That should be our goal, to be the breathing, living answer to that prayer. We have the chance to show the world God's perfect love, and that won't happen until we come together as the unified Body of Christ.

STUDY QUESTIONS

1. What are some of the biggest problems facing today's world? In what ways do you think division is feeding into those issues?

2. On a scale of 1-10, how unified is your team (1 being "in complete disarray," 10 being "unshakably unified")? Explain your answer.

3. What aspects of Jesus' team (the disciples, the apostles, the Early Church, etc.) do you find most interesting? Why?

4. What issues do you see within the modern Christian church? In what ways would you like to see Christians come together and become more unified?

5. What can you start doing today to help build unity within your church body or within your fellowship of believers?

11

~~~~~~

CHAPTER ELEVEN

THE
TEAM PICTURE

A Parable About Purpose

> **"I'll do whatever it takes to win games, whether it's sitting on a bench waving a towel, handing a cup of water to a teammate, or hitting the game-winning shot." – Kobe Bryant**

For some athletes, just being on the team is enough. Wearing the jersey and sitting on the bench is the prize.

The best teammates, however, are the ones who understand they have a role to play no matter how much of the game they get to play. They can contribute in practice. They can help make the team better. They might even have a chance to earn more playing time as they patiently and graciously wait for their opportunity.

That won't happen if an athlete is simply satisfied being on the team.

Perhaps NBA legend Kobe Bryant best summed it up when he described his attitude toward teamwork. When he was healthy, he was expected to make big plays and lead his Los Angeles Lakers club to victory.

His contributions didn't stop there. Even if he was taking a breather, Bryant was still "sitting on a bench waving a towel" to help cheer on his team. Or, in those times he was injured, he was "handing a cup of water" to his teammates.

Just being on the team was never an option. There was a greater purpose no matter the circumstance.

THE TEAM PICTURE

The University of Nebraska football team has historically been known for its walk-on program. Legendary head coach Tom Osborne was known for bringing up to 150 athletes to fall camp.

As one of Coach Osborne's assistants for 11 seasons, I had a first-hand look at the sea of football players that covered the field. For some reason, we usually took the team picture during the early days of preseason practice. Within a couple of weeks, however, a small number of the players would quit the team and our roster would end up closer to 110 players.

Years later, I would hear stories about former players telling prospective employers that they played for Nebraska. Even though they never stepped foot on the field or even made it through the preseason, the team picture was their proof that they were, in fact, a part of a prestigious program that would look good on anyone's resume.

On the other hand, the players who stayed weren't just happy to be in the team picture. They didn't stand around. They practiced. They worked hard. They made the rest of the team better. A number of walk-ons earned scholarships and became starters. Some, like Joel Mackovicka, even made the NFL. Others, like Scott Shanle and Sam Koch, won Super Bowl rings.

Those players didn't settle for just being on the team. They wanted to do more. They wisely believed they could make a difference, and that's exactly what they did.

FROM THE PALACE TO PURPOSE

The Old Testament is full of stories about men and women who had the choice to stay in their comfort zone or do something out of the ordinary in order to fulfill a greater purpose. Nehemiah was one who chose to do the latter. His story can be found in the book that bears his name.

There was really no good reason for Nehemiah to do anything spectacular with his life. He lived during a time when Judah was under

Persian control and lived in Persia, where he served as King Artaxerxes' cupbearer.

Nehemiah was likely pretty comfortable in the palace. It wasn't the perfect situation, but it wasn't terribly awful either. Everything changed, however, when Nehemiah found out his hometown of Jerusalem was facing a serious crisis. The city's walls were in a desperate state of disrepair, and the people were in grave danger.

Nehemiah jumped into action. No longer satisfied with his subservient role, he courageously approached the king and requested to be temporarily relieved of his duties so he could return home. This was a risky move, but it paid off. Artaxerxes sent Nehemiah back to Jerusalem and made him a provincial governor. The king also gave him access to resources and supplies.

It wasn't easy. Nehemiah had to fight opposition inside and outside of the city. He even had to ward off attacks from four nearby nations that sought to take advantage of the situation. Nehemiah, however, rose to the occasion and led an effort to rebuild Jerusalem's walls in an astounding 52 days.

Nehemiah went down in history as one of the Bible's great men of faith because he rejected a life of mediocrity and recognized the great potential God had placed within him. He wasn't satisfied with being in the team picture. Instead, Nehemiah left a legacy behind because he strove to fulfill a greater purpose.

A HIGHER CALLING

The number one reason Jesus died on the cross for your sins was so you could have a relationship with God the Father and have the promise of eternal life, but that wasn't all Jesus had in mind. His sacrifice made a way for you to be part of His team, a contributing member of something much bigger than you could ever imagine. What is that purpose? To be conformed to the image of Jesus Christ.

Like Nehemiah, we have a greater purpose. God is asking us to help Him build the Kingdom of God. He desires us to fulfill that purpose and invite others into His family. It's far more important than winning a game. The ramifications are literally the difference between life and death.

Here are some steps that will take you from the team picture and onto God's field of play.

1. Get to know Him. You need to reject the ways of this world and instead desire a closer relationship with God. That's how you'll gain the passion to fulfill His greater purpose for your life. This requires time spent in prayer, in the reading of God's Word, and in fellowship with other believers.

Come near to God and he will come near to you. Wash your hands, you sinners, and purify your hearts, you double-minded. (James 4:8)

2. Get to know yourself. See the value God has placed inside of you. Accept the fact that you have a place on His team and have important Kingdom work to do.

Each of you should use whatever gift you have received to serve others, as faithful stewards of God's grace in its various forms. (1 Peter 4:10)

3. Get out of your comfort zone. Don't let fear stop you from fulfilling your greater purpose. There's nothing anyone can say or do that can stop you from living out your calling, except yourself. That's because you have the almighty God, the Creator of the universe on your side.

"Have I not commanded you? Be strong and courageous. Do not be afraid; do not be discouraged, for the LORD your God will be with you wherever you go."

4. Get to work. Get off the bench. Be an active member of the team. Don't be okay with the status quo. Don't be comfortable with a mediocre life. There is fullness like nothing you've experienced before when you step into active duty for Christ.

Therefore, my dear brothers and sisters, stand firm. Let nothing move you. Always give yourselves fully to the work of the Lord, because you know that your labor in the Lord is not in vain. (1 Corinthians 15:58)

We can't afford to sit on the bench and be content to watch others do the work. It's all about proclaiming the gospel and leading the lost to Christ. This means shaking off the satisfaction of just being on the team, wearing the Christian jersey, and enjoying the eternal benefits of salvation.

Step out of the team picture and onto the playing field. This world needs you to be an active member of God's team!

STUDY QUESTIONS

1. What do you value most about being part of a team?

2. Have you ever been able to relate to the football players Coach Brown talked about who were happy to just be in the team picture? Why or why not?

3. Why do you think Nehemiah was compelled to risk his status in the palace in order to pursue a greater purpose? Have you ever found yourself in a similar situation?

4. Can you describe a time when you didn't feel like you were contributing to your team? What, if anything, did you do to change your situation?

5. Which of the four steps discussed have you been successful at taking? Which steps are you struggling to take, and how might taking those steps change your ability to fulfill a greater purpose?

12

CHAPTER TWELVE

~~~~~~

POCKET PRESENCE

A Parable About Evangelism

"If you panic in that pocket, you are no good." – Terry Bradshaw

Pocket presence. It's one of the most important attributes a quarterback should have—the ability to remain calm and poised in that area behind the line of scrimmage called the pocket.

Quarterbacks have to quickly assess the situation as soon as the ball is snapped on a passing play. Where is the offensive line protection? Where is the defensive pressure? Where are the open receivers? What is the exit strategy if everything falls apart?

Hall of Fame quarterback Terry Bradshaw understood the concept well. He knew poise was the key for any successful drop-back passer and used his pocket presence to lead the Pittsburgh Steelers to four Super Bowl titles.

"If you panic in that pocket," Bradshaw once said, "you are no good."

More recently, NFL fans have enjoyed Aaron Rodgers' masterful pocket presence. Not only is Rodgers one of the game's best pure passers, he's also been known to use his savvy footwork and movement in the pocket to get out of jams and pull off some spectacular plays. Some moments that come to mind include his three famous Hail Mary touchdowns and his iconic 8.3-second scramble drill that led to a key score in Green Bay's 2017 playoff victory against the New York Giants.

Rodgers would later explain to ESPN that his trademark ability to get out of trouble came from repetition in practice, which eventually led to a heightened sense of instinct.

"You learn the knack of pocket movements and presence and trying to keep two hands on the ball," he said, "and a set balance between looking for your exit spot and keeping your eyes downfield for a guy that's open for a touchdown."

POCKET PRESENCE

The quarterback is usually the highest paid player on any given NFL team for a reason. Along with the center, he touches the ball on every offensive play and has the most riding on his shoulders. The quarterback has to courageously stand in the pocket waiting to deliver the ball, even if a defender is breathing down his neck.

Pocket presence is of utmost importance no matter what scenario any given play might bring. For instance:

1. Quarterbacks must be aware of where their receivers are or where their routes are taking them.

2. Quarterbacks must be aware of the protection that's being provided.

3. Quarterbacks must be aware of the defensive scheme. What happens if the defense decides to bring an extra defender up to the line of scrimmage? What happens if the defense puts on a blitz? What happens if the defense drops an extra defender back into coverage and the receivers can't get open?

4. Quarterbacks must be aware of when to throw the ball. No matter the circumstance, he is constantly faced with pressure-packed decisions. The quarterback might need to break protection and scramble. He might need to throw the ball away.

Then, there are those times when a quarterback is under great duress and has no choice but to deliver that ball anyway. It's fourth down. There's a sense of urgency because the game is on the line.

5. Quarterbacks might need to take a hit. In some situations, throw-

ing the ball away or trying to force a completion is too risky. The best decision is to securely lock the ball and brace for the sack.

In each of those scenarios, the quarterback's teammates are looking to him for leadership. It's his job to remain calm, steadfast, and poised.

DELIVERING THE GOSPEL

Jesus has often been referred to as the Master Coach. For the sake of this parable, however, imagine that during His ministry Jesus was a quarterback, and the football was the gospel. His purpose was more than just winning games. Instead, Jesus had the enormous responsibility of delivering this eternity-altering message to the world.

Much like an actual quarterback, He was constantly aware of multiple factors and scenarios.

1) Jesus knew His receivers. Early in His ministry He found willing disciples that would be ready to listen to His words and believe His message. Conversely, Jesus knew there were those who weren't ready to hear that message.

2) Jesus knew His protections. Sometimes He could rely on help from His disciples, like the time they helped distribute food to the 5,000 (Matthew 14:13-21). More often, however, His protection came from God the Father and the Holy Spirit who strengthened Him amid Satan's attacks, like the temptation in the desert (Matthew 4:1-11) or the time of deep prayer in the Garden of Gethsemane leading up to Christ's crucifixion (Matthew 26:36-46).

3) Jesus was aware of the enemy's schemes. Satan used religious leaders, empirical rulers, and even members of Jesus' own team to try to stop the gospel from being delivered. He had to be deftly aware of who was for Him and who was against Him.

4) Jesus knew when to deliver the gospel. He took those opportunities as they came, like His approach of the woman at the well (John 4:1-26) or His unique interaction with Zacchaeus the tax collector (Luke 19:1-10).

Sometimes the timing wasn't right. For instance, the people of Gaderenes asked Him to leave town after He miraculously cast demons out of two men there (Matthew 8:28-34).

Jesus even faced His own fourth down. While nailed to the cross, He delivered the gospel to the thief as the end drew near (Luke 23:39-43).

5) Jesus was prepared to take a hit. The religious leaders conspired against Him, the Roman Empire feared Him, His disciple Judas betrayed Him, and ultimately the people who adored Him turned against Him. The latter days of His ministry were dangerous times and ultimately led to His death on the cross.

Praise God, we know that Jesus' crucifixion wasn't the end! After three days in the grave, Jesus made a comeback and won the ultimate victory over sin and death. In the days that followed, He reconnected with His disciples and commanded them to carry the gospel throughout the earth.

POISE UNDER PRESSURE

The Great Commission (Matthew 28:18-30) spurred a revolution that would change the world forever. Jesus essentially appointed each of them to be quarterbacks in their own right, to go out and deliver the gospel to all who might be willing to receive it. We too, as believers, are called to preach the Good News to those around us. Like Jesus, however, there are some things we need to do in order to be effective quarterbacks of the gospel.

1) Know your receivers. The Holy Spirit will alert you to opportunities to share God's Word with those around you such as your family, friends, co-workers or maybe random people that you meet in the store, on the street, on the bus, at the game or in the park.

2) Know your protections. If you aren't already, get plugged into a church where a pastor can teach you effective ways to deliver the gospel. Join a small group of believers that can help you sharpen your skills.

There are times, however, when you might have to go outside the normal protections. The government might be against you. Your own church or your Christian friends might not even be there to help. The apostle Paul was in that position many times and was forced to rely solely on the leading of the Holy Spirit. That's the most important thing to remember. Like Paul, it is imperative that you allow the Holy Spirit to be your protector and your guide.

3) Know your enemy's schemes. Satan wants nothing more than to keep the gospel from being delivered to a lost and dying world. He will try to distract you with the cares of life. He will try to tempt you to chase material dreams. He will try to slow you down with fear and doubt. He will try to make you feel incompetent, unprepared and unworthy of the calling. These are all lies and can be dispelled with God's promises.

For the Spirit God gave us does not make us timid, but gives us power, love and self-discipline. (2 Timothy 1:7)

4) Know your circumstances. You don't shout and scream when you are in the library, in a classroom, or at a funeral. On the other hand, you might make some noise when you're at a sporting event, a concert, or a party.

The same is true for the believer delivering the gospel. Not every circumstance is the appropriate venue or the right time. Sometimes you have to wait until you've developed a trusting relationship first or wait until they are prepared to receive the Good News.

Other times you have to wait until the Holy Spirit prompts you to share eternal truths. There might even be times when you make an attempt and get shut down. That's when you just lock the gospel away and wait to share it another day.

Then there are those fourth down moments where it's time to get rid of the ball no matter what. What do you do when a person who has rejected Jesus his or her whole life is now on their deathbed? You've got to make a play. You've got to deliver the gospel.

5) Know the consequences. There are times when you might need to share the gospel under incredible duress. It could cost you a job, your reputation, or your standing in the community. Some Christians are even risking their very lives as they evangelize unbelievers in places where religious freedom is non-existent. Like them, we must be prepared to take a hit just like Jesus was willing to take the ultimate hit for us on the cross.

STUDY QUESTIONS

1. On a scale of 1-10, how would you rate how effectively you are delivering the gospel (1 being "cold as ice," 10 being "on fire for God")?

2. What are some ways you might be able to personally discern who is and who isn't ready to receive the gospel?

3. As someone called to deliver the gospel, what protections do you have in place as you fulfill that calling?

4. What are some schemes the enemy is trying to use in order to keep you from sharing the gospel with others?

5. What are some things you can start doing today that will help you be better prepared to deliver the gospel?